MW01439428

WORDS TO BELIEVE
AND *FEEL*

WORDS THAT DEFINE WHO PEOPLE ARE

MY JOURNEY TO ANSWER MY SON'S QUESTION:

'DAD, WHAT ELSE DO YOU BELIEVE?'

Personal stories of a simple guy from Deer Isle, Down East Maine.
From a dad for his kids.

For a PDF E-Book version visit: www.wordstobelieve.com or www.Lulu.com
All net profits from this E-Book will be donated to Maine Behavioral Healthcare
Thank you for saving, and rebuilding, lives.

'The only true wisdom is in knowing you.'
Socrates

Copyright © 2023 by Leigh Canfield
All rights reserved.

PROLOQUE
WHAT THIS BOOK IS ABOUT

Personal Stories of a simple guy from Deer Isle, Down East Maine

Many years ago, my son asked me a tough question: 'Dad, what else do you believe?' I couldn't answer it, and so began writing short stories to answer his question for him, and for me. For some unknown reason, I have found writing to be therapeutic, urges me to clarify feelings, and enlightens in some way. Many of these stories were born along the shores and islands of Eggemoggin Reach, which borders the western shores of Deer Isle, Down East Maine.

I decided to consolidate some of them to put together a little book which tries to wrap my arms around a theme from all those teachings of the great books and wise men, perhaps best described by a quote from the most influential philosopher of his time, whose name was Aristotle:

'Knowing yourself is the beginning of all wisdom.'

It is the most consistent theme integrated in all revered teachings.

That is what this simple book is mostly about...

Together with thoughts, guided in part by me writing this book, on ways to move grief and heartache to soften, rather than harden, a heart.

'Home is not a place; it is a feeling.'
Cecelia Ahern

A GUIDE TO AN INTERNAL COMPASS
WE ALL YEARN TO FEEL

From a dad for his kids

I live in a state called Maine,

and a good part of the time at my sacred spot, which they call Down East Maine.

Since I was a kid, it has always been the place

I can feel

and be me.

I'm just a simple guy from Deer Isle, Down East Maine.

Many of my stories were born or written on the ledges or islands within Eggemoggin Reach - a 15-mile stretch of beautiful waters between Deer Isle, Down East Maine and the mainland - where the towns of Brooksville, Sedgwick, and Brooklin, Maine were settled, and now lay.

For Brendan, Erik, and Anushka

ARISTOTLE'S WISDOM

'The most important relationship we can all have is the one you have with yourself.

The most important journey you can take is one of self-discovery.

To know yourself, you must spend time with yourself,

you must not be afraid to be alone.

Knowing yourself is the beginning of all wisdom.'

Aristotle
*Ancient Greek philosopher and scientist, whose mentor was Plato,
and who was one of the greatest intellectual figures of Western history*

'Your vision will become clear only when you can look
into your own heart. Who looks outside, dreams;
who looks inside, awakes.'
Carl Jung

PRELUDE TO STORIES

TOPIC	PAGE
Background	11
Purpose	12-15
Who am I?	16-19
Mentoring	20-21
Grief and Enlightenment	22-23
It's about what you Feel	24-25
The Daydream *What if?*	26-29

'At the center of your being you have the answer,
once you know who you are.'
Lao Tzu

BACKGROUND

Many years ago, my son innocently asked me a tough when I shared my feelings about the importance of being honest and kind.

After a long pause, he then asked me:

"Dad, what else do you believe?"

And I knew, really, at that moment, he was asking me: 'Who am I?'

I actually stuttered, and was self-embarrassed, and changed the topic to the Boston Bruins, which he and I knew all the answers to.

But it bothered me so much I began writing down some answers to his question that same night.

I thought of simple words, and found that a single word, in the right context, and shared by real stories, may provide a tool to guide.

And as I was defining my words and writing my stories, I understood I was writing it not only for him, but also mostly for me.

There is, in my mind, no more important [and answerable] question, because it answers one of the most meaningful questions ever asked: Who am I?'

Because when you are able to effortlessly and comfortably express what you truly believe and feel, *out-loud and clear*, you will know who you are….

and then, this world, becomes your world.

'Live your purpose and make your soul smile.'
Frank Sonnenberg

PURPOSE

The purpose of this book was to answer my son's question, share how it changed me in meaningful ways, and helped instill an internal compass that helps guide.

And so, after much reflection and work, I had answered his question, for me.

And at what I felt was the right moment, I reminded my son of his question he had asked me awhile back. Although he didn't remember, I told him I wanted to now share my answer with him anyway.

I began by sharing that quote in a book of wisdom called Proverbs which served as a guide and remains in my thoughts:

'Whatever a person thinketh in his heart, so is he.'

And because I had done my work, and practiced, and knew inside and out the words that had embedded a natural moral compass within, the words flowed gently from my mouth, like water in a slow-moving calm country stream.

I could tell that he was listening. and when I was done, I felt relieved, at peace, and whole - knowing I had done what I felt I was obligated to do. To share my Words and compass within which leads me each and every minute of each and every day.

I knew deep down these are the most important and perhaps difficult things a parent can teach and share – that nothing else comes even close.

As I looked at him, I had this vision that he may at some time also take what I had shared, add some of his own Words to Believe, and ingrain his own internal compass into his soul to guide and lead.

And my vision expanded when I imagined he may also pass down those similar things to his children, and they to theirs.

And so, one purpose of this book was to leave a family heirloom of sorts, to always be there, and help guide my children, and theirs.

And another purpose was to provide a guide on how to confidently articulate a memorable answer when asked:

Who are you?

'The only person you are destined to become,
is the person you decide to be.'
Ralph Waldo Emerson

To be able to say it - out loud and clear.

Since so few can.

If you have a need or vision to share your Words to Believe, and your personal compass with your children, or others, and perhaps leave a family heirloom of sorts of your own, I hope my writings may provide some ideas to help you know and share those answers, in your own way, for you, and all of yours.

Leigh

'To find yourself, think for yourself.'
Socrates

'WHO AM I ?'

Ramana Maharshi, Indian sage

As human beings, we all yearn for our lives to matter. We are all made for a purpose and have a hunger to define what that is. From the day we are born, we are taught how to read, write, do math, and learn history and biology. And thousands of things more. In the beginning it seems all so overwhelming, but we find when we focus, and practice, we learn over time.

Although this learning is invaluable, I have found that we are rarely challenged to explore inward.

And perhaps the most meaningful question of all may have been posed by the South Indian sage Ramana Maharshi - who ministered peace and self-awareness - and challenged all to answer his simple question:

'Who am I?'

Some argue it is just a trick question, and not answerable. But that is not true. It is a meaningful question, and because we learn from teachings of wise men and sacred books, we know, at least directionally, the answer.

'We are whatever we thinketh in our heart.'

That is who we are. A person needs to define what they believe, to know what is in their heart. Therein lies the beginning of the answer.

What do you believe? Or more precisely, since it comes from the heart, what do you feel?

Like anything, the answer to this question takes time and effort, but challenges us in very personal ways. We will need to do a lot of reflection, selective reading, and soul-searching. Some, like me, may find nature to be good grounds.

We must reflect and examine again and again, until we finally know it feels about right, and good for us. We must do this by ourselves, completely on our own. I have learned that just going to Church, is not enough – but was never meant to be.

'The only journey is the journey within.'
Rainer Mariah Rilke

Over time, as with most things, I slowly learned that simple is normally clear and best and found one way to define your beliefs is to visualize important simple words that illuminate the values within your conscience and heart, define them simply, feel them deeply, and over time embed them deep inside and within.

And once you do that work and feel you have prioritized your core words and know what is in your heart, you must learn how to articulate that, and practice. *Because until you can clearly articulate something, you don't really know it.* Your words must be imbedded into your brain and soul.

And once that happens, you will be able to comfortably share what you believe *and feel* with others, which you may yearn to do. I have seen that it surprises and even shocks people when you are able to articulate this clearly.

Since so few can.

And so, when you see someone being bullied or mistreated, you will stand up, speak, and protect, rather than turn your head and pretend you don't see.

Because the word 'Empathy' is now ingrained into your brain and soul - together with words like Faith, Forgiveness, Honesty, Character, Trust, and Truth – which serve as the basis of your sacred compass to point and guide you right and clear.

And, importantly, once your Words are embedded within, you also gain the courage to stand against words that conflict with your beliefs; words like bullying, lying, cruelty, unforgiving, and greed.

Standing against something you oppose means you are standing up for something you believe. And there are times a person needs to stand for what is right, even if it means you may at times stand alone.

The world suffers not only because of acts of bad people, but also, and more importantly, the silence of good people.

Because silence offers and breeds consent.

And so, when it comes to your sacred values, reflected by the core Words you Believe, I urge all

to never be silent, and never consent.

Leigh

'A mentor is someone who allows you to see the hope within yourself.'
Oprah Winfrey

MENTORING

Although I am a bit embarrassed sharing things so personal, I am glad I have. I am now able to articulate what I believe, and who I am, and my writings may be [just] one model for my kids and others to use and integrate into their lives over time.

But I have a need to say that every parent knows the truth when it comes to guiding our children, or others of any kind.

Although it is important what we say, and write, and what we say and write can certainly impact and guide in very positive ways, that is not theirs, or others, guiding light.

Those are not the driving examples for which they yearn.

For every minute they listen to what a person may say or may write, there are 10,000 minutes they watch how a person lives.

The driving examples for which they yearn, and which we all seek, are models on how to live a life.

They will follow how we act, feel, treat others, and what we do.

They will watch, and follow the example of how a person lives their life, day by each day.

Those are the people I viewed as my most revered mentors during my lifetime, and sense most feel the same way.

If you truly live your life based on the Words you choose to believe, embrace your internal compass to lead and guide, and live your life the way you always imagined it could and should be lived…

They may too.

Leigh

'Those who are bereaved and grieve are not alone.
We belong to the largest company in all the world –
the company of all those who have known suffering.'
Helen Keller

GRIEF AND ENLIGHTENMENT

'Grief and love are forever intertwined.'
Nick Cave

There will be times in this life when very difficult things may happen to us, or those we love, and suffering and grief may overwhelm; especially when painful things happen to family members – those with whom there is unconditional love.

Although I will not share details, I have lived through a good deal of that, and was slowly able to manage my grief to soften, rather than harden, my heart. Mostly because over time I was able to imbed the Words faith, love, and hope into my being and heart.

I urge others who may inevitably go through grief and pain, to diligently resist your heart to harden.

The sacred books and wise men teach that only suffering and darkness will bring out a great light.

Although I never understood or even believed this when younger, I have found the connection between grief and enlightenment to be very real for me.

I think that may be because those who have experienced deep grief and suffering are enlightened with this word called empathy.

A uniquely human trait that enables a person to look into the eyes of others who are in pain,

and genuinely see and feel themselves, or others they love.

And that alone will not only change your life,

but also all those you touch.

Leigh

'Mankind is governed by feelings, not reason.'
Samuel Adams

*'The best and most beautiful things in the world cannot be seen,
or even touched. They must be felt with the heart...'*
Helen Keller

IT'S ABOUT WHAT YOU FEEL

As I was writing my stories, I came to realize that I hadn't really instilled my words into my brain and soul when I was younger and in times past. And I sometimes felt moments of deep regret. I wish I had known then what I know now. But am also grateful I now know, what I know now.

Even though these words are now imbedded within me, and I do feel much better about who I am and me, I am still a person with many flaws.

But I do feel much more at peace – and this journey of sorts has changed the way I live, act, treat others, and feel – while also impacting how others may view me.

I just feel inside I am a better person, since I now have this clear compass ingrained within.

As I defined my words and wrote my stories, I slowly learned that 'Words' have different 'depths.'

There is a difference between defining a word, believing in a word, and *feeling* a word. And I slowly began to understand that a person can only engrain a word into their heart and soul if they genuinely and deeply *feel* that word.

A person may believe in a word called Love, but believing in Love, and feeling Love, are different. We must really *feel* Love, in order to embed it our 'heart.'

We must *feel* Kindness to instill it in our being; not just say we believe in it.

We must *feel* Forgiveness, to ingrain it in our soul.

We must *feel* Gratefulness, to root it deep inside.

We must *feel* that word called Character, to ground it into our brain.

We must *feel* Hope, to never ever let it go.

And we must *feel* Faith, to have Him feel us. Saying a prayer, and deep praying, are completely different things.

And so, my words and stories were intended to provide a guide to at least try to help some feel, rather than just believe.

Because we need to really feel something, to live it.

Your compass should not just be about the Words, but the feelings within them.

Leigh

'I dream my painting and I paint my dream.'
Vincent Willem van Gogh

WHAT IF

'THE DAYDREAM'

'You must be the change you wish to see.'
Mahatma Ghandi

'Everything starts as somebody's daydream.'
Larry Niven

THE DAYDREAM

I had a little daydream the other day.

Just a little daydream from a simple guy from Deer Isle, Down East Maine.

I wondered what the world may be like if everyone tried to answer this simple, yet important and meaningful question: Who am I? - inspired by an Indian sage.

What if instead of spending all our time studying and reflecting only on all our classes and crafts, we added this meaningful subject to the list?

What if it was the first subject we studied and was a class required for all to take; so each person in this world was urged to define their own words to live by, which would describe what they believed and who they are; and which would instill a compass to guide how they live, act, treat others, and feel?

What if we learned that this was certainly an answerable question, and that most people in the world came up with similar words that reflect principles like character, honesty, empathy, and faith.

What if there was a form that every politician was required to complete - where they were asked to gnaw and gnaw and come up with their own honest answers on the Words they Believed and required to share – so others could rightly cast their votes.

What if all the good people of this world had the courage to live and share the Words they Believe - and embrace the ballot to shut down Words that shun.

And what if this all started with all the good people of this world, which is surely the most people of this world, answering that simple [and certainly answerable] three-word question:

Who am I?

Which may, perhaps, help us answer that ultimate human question: Who are *we*?

What if all this happened? How might the world change?

How might, or could, it be?

Just a little daydream from a simple guy from Deer Isle, Down East Maine.

'There is no greater power on this earth
than a story'

Libra Bray

REAL STORIES

OF MY WORDS TO BELIEVE, AND FEEL

'Knowing yourself is the beginning of all Wisdom.'
Aristotle

These stories are intended to paint a picture of sorts of Words to Believe which I have chosen to engrain into my brain and soul, to help visualize and feel what those words may really mean.

Knowing that the most important words may be Love, Faith, and Hope,

'Only three things will last forever—faith, hope, and love—and the greatest of these is love.'
Corinthians: 13:13

'Those who tell the stories rule the world.'
Native American proverb

YOUR QUESTION:

'Dad, what else do you believe?'

?

MY ANSWER:

'Whatever a person thinketh in his heart, so is he.'
Proverbs

I believe in, feel, and am

These Words

'Our stories are the tellers of us.'
Cliff Clive

STORIES

I believe in:	Story	Page
Love	Unconditional Love	36-39
Hope	Homemade Lemonade	40-45
Empathy	See You	46-51
Poise	Al Clayton	52-57
Faith	Never Lonely	58-63
Wonderful	Wonderful Tonight	64-71
Happiness	Blueberries	72-75
The Truth	The Truth	76-79
Giving	Giving	80-85
Forgiveness	The Forgiveness Tree	86-91
Overcome	Lou Paulmier	92-97
Gratitude	Roger Randal and Sons	98-101
Character	John Tulp	102-107
Kindness	Bob Lemieux	108-113
Family	Bucket	114-119
Work	Jeff Bunt	120-127
Courage	Travis Roy	128-133
Friendship	Chip	134-139
Honesty	Honesty: A Mindset	140-143
Trust	Trusting You	144-147
Purpose	Buck	148-153
Your Question	My Answer	154-161

More to come

'Love cures people'
Karl Menninger, American psychiatrist, and author

BELIEVE IN

LOVE

'Love is all there, really, is'
Mother Teresa

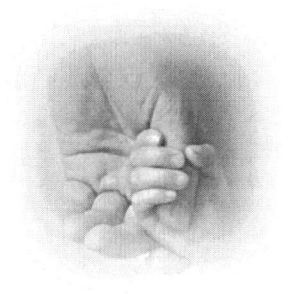

Definition: a profoundly tender affection for another person.

'Love is patient, love is kind. It does not envy, it does not boast, it is not proud. It does not dishonor others, it is not self-seeking, it is not easily angered, it keeps no record of wrongs. Love does not delight in evil but rejoices with the truth. It always protects, trusts, hopes, and perseveres.'
Corinthians

'It's not how much we give, but how much love we put into giving.'
Mother Teresa

UNCONDITIONAL LOVE

I walked into our home, after a long day at work. It was about 5:30. Leslie was holding Brendan, our newborn son, in her arms. Our first child. Our eldest. Tears in her eyes. He was 2 months old.

He had gone in for a check-up. There was something different about his left eye. The doctor said it was a thing called PHPV. An extremely rare birth condition which they did not catch at birth. A condition which would require surgery and mean permanent blindness in his left eye.

At first, I did not understand. Then, for a moment, didn't accept. I kept my fear, my pain, hidden. Not knowing what to say, I tried to comfort her, saying it would be fine. I gently took him from her arms and held him in mine. I told him, like her, all was going to be OK. I walked around the house, holding him, not knowing where to go. Wandering. masking my pain. Asking God to guide me through my pain.

I went outside and held him carefully in my arms. Rocking him gently. Looking at his face. Staring. Tears in my eyes; tears I would not show. Trying to be strong. The pain so deep. The feeling so strong. The love so real.

Knowing completely a term I had heard my whole life, but did not fully understand, until I heard him cry, out from the womb.

At that moment, knowing completely a term called Unconditional Love.

The feeling of feelings.

A love so deep, it is integrated into every inch of your body. Every ounce of your spirit. Every measure of your soul. Imbedded in your heart: complete, absolute, supreme. The type no one can ever take away. A feeling so deep, you would gladly give up your eyes, your limbs, your life; in less than a second.

The feeling I have for each one of my children. The feeling every single parent knows.

The feeling that God graciously gave us, to feel.

Leigh

'We judge a man's wisdom by his hope.'
Ralph Waldo Emerson

BELIEVE IN

HOPE

'Hope is a waking dream.'
Aristotle

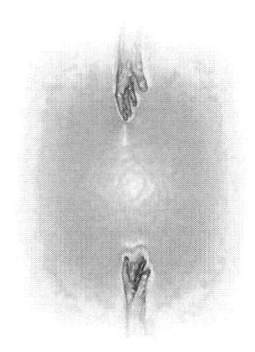

Definition: feeling that what is wanted can be had or that events will turn out for the best.

'Hope is the heartbeat of the soul.'
Michelle Horst

WORD TO BELIEVE: HOPE

HOMEMADE LEMONADE

There are times in this life when we are given a lemon. The lemon isn't expected. It is big and very sour. It is overwhelming. It is excruciatingly painful. It isn't fair.

It is like you have been thrown out of a spaceship. You are all alone and completely lost, floating aimlessly and helplessly. You are in that deep vast black space, looking for any ray of light – any ray of hope.

We may ask others to help. But others aren't always able to help, no matter how you and they may try and try and try and try.

And we slowly and painfully accept that the pain can't be solved from others. It can't be bought, and no one can take that helplessness, hopelessness, and pain away.

Except you.

We come to realize deep down that we need to do it completely on our own. We don't even know what 'it' is, but we need to take the helm, and control. We need to find and use all our inner courage and strength somehow. And never give up hope – because it is all we have.

And, as the sacred books teach, we may learn how suffering may bring a type of enlightenment.

And if we really want and try - we find that there may be a way to slowly churn that sour lemon into a type of lemonade – which changes its taste. And after a while, we may be able to churn it into something better, something we would never expect.

And then a miracle may happen; and that lemonade over time may end up tasting sweet.

We learn that if we hold on to hope, and muster all our inner courage and strength, we can turn that painful lemon into our own sweet fresh-squeezed homemade lemonade. It is different, but also good.

And along the way we slowly become enlightened that it needs to start and center on

Faith, Love, and Hope.

Those only things that last forever; and seared on my leg.

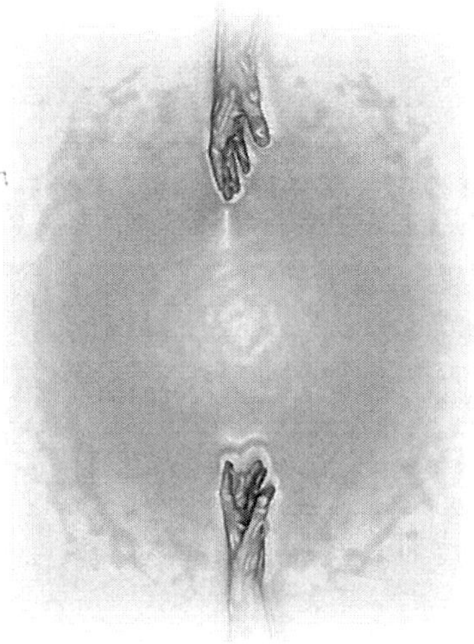

When you are given that sour lemon, filled with overwhelming pain, are all alone and lost, feel helpless and hopeless, are floating aimlessly, and looking for any ray of light....

I hope you are able to embrace your inner courage and strength, to find, and make,

your own fresh-squeezed

homemade lemonade.

Leigh

'Seek first to understand, then to be understood.'
Steven Covey, American author

BELIEVE IN

EMPATHY

"The great gift of human beings is the power of empathy."
Meryl Streep

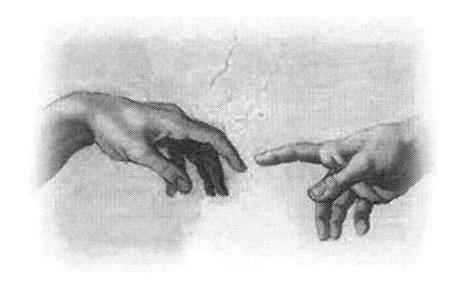

Definition: the psychological identification with or vicarious experiencing of the emotions or thoughts of another.

'When you start to develop your powers of empathy,
the whole world opens up to you.'
Susan Sarandon

SEE YOU

When I was younger, about 19 or so, I was walking along a street, in Minneapolis, in the late fall. The sun was shining a bright shine. And through that shine, I saw what I thought was a man. From a distance, standing on a corner.

As I slowly got closer, step by step, I began to make out that his shoulders were a bit slumped over, and his clothes seemed to be torn.

Getting closer, by each step, I noticed his face from a distance. It seemed tired. And his half-beard was a bit grey.

And something seemed familiar.

His shirt was ripped where it came down to his wrists, and his worn gloves were open at the fingertips. He his pants were too short. They didn't come down to his ankles.

And as I got closer, I could see he was holding a cardboard sign. "Will work for Food." Holding it tightly to his chest. With a tin cup at his feet. As I began closing in on that corner to cross the street,

I made eye contact with the man. And something seemed familiar.

As I reached the corner, I had to stop for traffic. And I stood next to him. Less than a foot away.

I looked over at him. And he at me. Being young, and not knowing better, I said Hi. And he smiled a tired very little smile. And nodded a little nod. As if to say Thank You. For just saying Hi.

And I saw something familiar.

There were tired wrinkles along his forehead. And the clothes were dirty. Like he had worn them for a year. His hair was all ruffled, like it hadn't ever been washed. And his coat was open, because there were no buttons.

And as I looked into his eyes, I felt this something inside me. Because the eyes, despite everything else, were kind.

But as I looked into his eyes, they seemed soft. There was something in his eyes. Tired, sad. They were a bit moist. Maybe a bit glazed. And the sunlight was reflecting upon them. I sensed a hopelessness, still clinging to hope.

'It takes courage to feel empathy.'
Maya Angelou

I reached into my pocket, and emptied my change, which was all I had. And put it in the tin cup, at his feet. Without saying a word.

I looked up again, and saw his tired, but genuine, little smile. And I looked again into his moist, somewhat glazed, eyes.

And recognized what was familiar.

I saw a reflection in his eyes, from the sunlight. And in that reflection,

I saw me.

I hope when you see a man in the street, with broken clothes and heart…

You see you.

Leigh

'Lone eagles, soaring in the clouds, fly with silent, peaceful poise,
While turkeys, in their earth-bound crowds,
fill the atmosphere with noise.'
William Arthur Ward, American writer and author

BELIEVE IN

POISE

Definition: a dignified, self-confident manner or bearing; composure; self-possession.

'Poise is the earmark of mental strength.'
Preston Nolan

AL CLAYTON

There I was. Sitting on a tree stump, on the banks of the Allagash River. One of the most majestic rivers in Maine. I was 18 years old.

It was getting to be dusk, and the sun was beginning to set. It reflected, orange, off the glass water.

But I didn't notice. I noticed the mosquitoes, the size of bees. With stingers, like needles. There were a billion of them. I was swatting them, jerking my head, trying to clap them all to death. They were going up my nose, in my ears, attached to my face.

I looked around, and saw everyone else, all doing the same thing. Frenetic; swatting, clapping, moving around to try to escape them. Tears in our eyes.

And then I saw him. He was sitting in the middle of us all. At a picnic table. Admiring the sunset, taking in the reflection of the sun. Watching a fish or two jump up. Watching the ripples they made.

He was an accomplished musician, of Quaker faith. A teacher, and counselor. He had been my counselor for so many years. But he was so much more. The type of man whose youngest son was supposedly born 'mentally challenged,' but who is now beautifully married, completely employed, and maybe smarter than me.

A lesson on hope, courage, and poise, he taught us all. By watching, just watching, how he lived his life. Principled, graceful, egoless, serene, assured. A man who knew so well what was inside.

The mosquitoes were hovering around his head. Maybe a million of them; but, somehow, they were not *on* him.

I noticed one come upon his cheek. He slowly moved up his right hand, and gently brushed it off his face, with his index finger. It slowly fluttered away.

Hoping some of his magic may wear off on me, I went over to sit with him. "The mosquitoes are bad tonight," I said.

He looked at me, gently brushed another aside, and responded, nicely, "Well, yes, but they have as much right to be here as you or me."

'Poise is Power'
Confucius

He again looked up to the river, admiring what was there for us all to see.

After a couple minutes, the others drifted over to sit with us. All six of us now. Near him, no longer swatting. Gently brushing.

Looking at the river, admiring what was there to see.

Another lesson, without him even knowing.

Leigh

'Faith is like a bird that feels dawn breaking and sings while it is still dark.'
Scandinavian Proverb

BELIEVE IN

FAITH

"You can do very little with faith, but you can do nothing without it.'
Samuel Butler

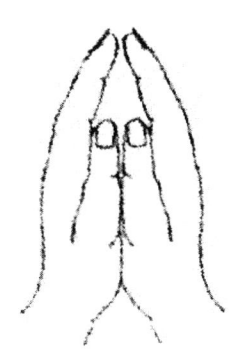

Definition: confidence, trust, or believe in something greater than you that can't be proven.

'You can do very little with faith, but you can do nothing without it.'
Samuel Butler, English writer

NEVER LONELY

On this journey of life, I have slowly found Faith as the best of friends. Although I do share this with some at times, like I am right now with you, I have no desire to convince others; since I know it is something a person needs to feel for and with themselves, from within. But I will share that I do believe in this feeling most call God, and something much greater than me.

When it comes to a belief in something greater than me, or us, I have come to believe a person should not rely on this thing called 'reason.' That reason is replaced by a word called 'Faith,' knowing that Faith, by definition, is something which cannot be 'proven' in any way.

My faith has evolved over time by reflecting, feeling nature, learning from the teachings of the world's wise men, and readings of the sacred books – knowing full well some may twist, bend, and abuse the words for their personal selfish gains. But, in the end, and partly for that reason, it is my conscience, Gods voice within, which always rules. I have learned there may be different ways to reach for Him, at different moments and times. Jesus has served as one pathway for me during very meaningful times. And nature is one of my sacred healing grounds.

Over time, I have come to believe that there is one God with many names, and those are the names of every one of us. For me, then, there is one God inside eight billion names. He is not a 'thing', out there in never-where - but rather a special and sacred 'feeling' deep within. And feelings are very, very real. Much more than things.

Since Feelings last, and things don't. And so when I feel God, I genuinely feel, he feels me.

There are certainly moments when I need to 'let go, and let God,' and ask and wait for Him, to come up and out, somehow. It occurs during good times, reflective times, and very difficult times. Since grief drives a person to deep reflection and softens one's heart.

Like when we were told Brendan was blind in one eye. Or when Erik had a head injury and needed lifesaving surgery. Or my mother living with Alzheimer's. Or when Leslie was diagnosed with Parkinson's disease.

I have learned there is a big difference between praying, and saying a prayer.

'My faith is God is complete, so I am unafraid:'
William Farrow

Although no one knows what may happen when we pass, I genuinely feel if you feel that feeling called 'God,' both before and during that moment you pass, he will feel you.

And if you both feel each other, he will love you, hold you, and take care of you in ways no one can know.

But it will be based on that word called Love.

That is what I feel, and define as my 'Faith.'

My faith has somehow enlightened me, altered my Purpose, and helps guide me each day.

So when I am at my favorite quiet spot, where I can hear nothing but the wind, or the tide, or chirping, of some kind. Where the hills can be seen, or the sun can rise, I feel my conscience, God's sacred voice within, as he asks to come up – from deep inside – and out.

It is pure. It is real. It is honest. I am at Peace.

All alone.

But in no way lonely.

Leigh

'For there are only these three things that endure: Faith, Hope and Love,
but the greatest of these is Love.'
Corinthians

'Wonder is the first of all the passions.'
René Descartes

BELIEVE IN

WONDER
AND THAT WORD WONDERFUL

'Wonder is the beginning is Wisdom.'
Aristotle

'To Wonder is to be curious, and the greatest virtue of man is perhaps curiosity.'
Anatole France

Definition: to be filled with curiosity, admiration, amazement, or awe.

'He who can no longer pause to wonder and stand rapt in awe,
has eyes closed.'
Mark Twain

WONDERFUL TONIGHT

We were in the living room, getting ready to have dinner with some friends, and she asked me to help her put on this white silk scarf. She couldn't reach far enough to tuck it in, so I walked over to help her tuck it in just right. I was behind her, and she asked me how it looked.

My eyes became moist, and I told her she looked

'Wonderful Tonight.' Those words from my favorite Erik Clapton song.

I wouldn't let her see my eyes moisten. So, I stayed behind her for a bit, knowing that I have never told her enough, that Wonderful isn't only the way she looks - but the way she is.

And at that moment standing behind her with my hands on her shoulders, and with unseen moistened eyes, I reminisced.

I remembered so well that day 39 years ago, when I was standing in line at this little ice cream shop in a small Village called Yarmouth Village, Maine. I was there with a friend, on a beautiful blue sky summer day. And then, just like that, I saw her.

She was in front of me about 15 feet or so. She turned around to talk to her friend, and I saw those beautiful eyes. I could sense she was soft spoken, and she seemed shy. Amazingly, my friend knew her friend somehow. I walked over to introduce myself, I got her name, which was Leslie – a beautiful name - and I was never the same.

As I was standing behind her tucking her scarf in with my hands on her shoulders, I reminisced about all the memories we have had between that day 39 years ago, and that moment right then. All those memories were remembered in only these few short moments.

My eyes moistened again, and a tear dropped from my right eye. I quickly wiped it away so no one would see.

She slowly turned around and quietly asked me how the tucked in scarf looked, And I told her again, it and she looked

'Wonderful Tonight.'

Because she did and was.

'Time has a wonderful way of showing you what really matters.'
Dr. Susan Bali Haass

She nodded her head as if to accept that the scarf now looked good, and then slowly moved toward her jacket on the chair, to begin to slowly put her white winter jacket on.

And as I looked at her, I felt how much I have always loved, and love, her. And regret not letting her know that nearly as often as I should.

Although, like most families, we have been through challenging times, and have dealt with grief, we have weathered the ups and downs. And when there have been problems, even if unintentional, I know they were almost always caused by me.

I thought how loyal, sensitive, fragile, and caring she is. And how she put up with this 'workaholic' at times. With me working at two jobs, a full-time job - and building a business much more than on the side. Unaware, that I was too busy, being too busy, too often and many times. And her dealing with those warts of mine. Knowing her freckles have soothed my many warts so many times.

And what a great mother she is and has been, of those three great children of ours. Brendan, Erik, and Anushka. As Brendan has said since he was four, 'She is the greatest Mom in the whole wide world.' Which is just a fact, and True.

And I thought how lucky I have been to be with Leslie this long, and knowing how much I loved and love her, and not saying that she looked and was

'Wonderful Tonight,' more often or times.

And that may be why I have this deep need to write this story, about and for her.

After she put her jacket on, she slowly took her medicine. And as we walked out the door, I held her left hand and put my other hand on her shoulder to steady her, to help her down our granite steps leading to the car. Slowly, to make sure she didn't slip, or lose her balance, one small step at a time.

Over time she has had difficulty walking, and her mouth may quiver, and her legs may shake, but she moves ahead. There are things she can no longer do, but things she still can do. And she never complains. Because she is who she is, which is wonderful.

She will not let the Parkinson's, which was diagnosed 6 years ago, control her. Rather, we will do our best to control it, and our lives. Knowing that being alive, no matter what the obstacles, is loving being alive. And that we should relish and enjoy each moment, and laugh out-loud at least once each day. And that we will never, ever, let go of hope.

And so, as I was tucking in her scarf to make it fit right, my eyes moistened and a tear fell from my right eye, because I felt how lucky I was to be able to say those words that she looked and was

'Wonderful Tonight.'

And to know and feel I have been so lucky to be with someone like Leslie. Someone I love more today,

than that day 39 years ago, when I first saw her in that ice cream stand line.

So please know, I have always loved you,

And will never stop loving you.

To and for me, you have been and will always be

My only 'Wonderful Tonight.'

Leigh

Shared as a Mother's Day gift.

'Make happy those who are near, and those who are far will come.'
Chinese Proverb

BELIEVE IN

HAPPINESS

*'Go confidently in the direction of your dreams,
Live the life you always imagined'**
Henry David Thoreau

Definition: Feeling of good fortune; pleasure; contentment; joy.

'Happiness: Don't pursue it, create it.'
Ralph Waldo Emerson

BLUEBERRIES

I love blueberries. They taste so good.

The other day I bought 2 cartons of fresh Maine blueberries. I put them in the refrigerator and was looking forward to eating at least some of them - later that day.

I thought about eating them a couple hours later - but thought I would wait longer. I didn't want to eat them all right then. I didn't want to waste them right then and there - so I waited.

I thought about eating them that night, but thought I should wait longer, for some unknown reason. Thinking that the longer I wait, the better they may taste.

I thought about eating them that next morning, but again, didn't want to enjoy them right then. I wanted to wait for a better moment for that enjoyment. Because they taste so good.

Well, after a while, I had forgotten that I had bought those great blueberries and put them in the refrigerator.

And by the time I remembered several days later, I opened up the refrigerator and saw that they were all brownish, dried up, and spoiled.

And I got so mad at me.

I was never able to enjoy them. I had wasted all that enjoyment by waiting for a moment that I thought may be better and tastier.

But that moment never came.

Lately, as I am now older, I have decided to not waste those blueberries anymore.

When I want to go skiing, I don't wait. When I want to play tennis, I don't wait. When I want to call a friend. I don't wait. When I want to go fishing, or canoeing, or kayaking, or just jump in the ocean, I don't wait. Or when I want to show someone that I love them – show is better than tell -
I no longer wait.

Not only is there no reason to wait, it is bad to wait. Because if you wait too long, you will miss out on so many beautifully sweet tasting things in this life.

And you will be so mad,

at you. Leigh

'All truths are easy to understand once they are discovered,
the point is to discover them.'
Galileo Galilei

BELIEVE IN

THE TRUTH

'The Truth shall make you free.'
Martin Luther King

Definition: the true or actual state of a matter; an indisputable fact, proposition, or principle.

'And ye shall know the Truth, and the Truth shall make you free.'
The Bible [John 8:32]

THE TRUTH

I have come to believe that the most important things in life are simple.

And the one of the most important words to believe is what I call 'The Truth:'

'Whatever you give out, you will get back.'

It is the core teachings of all the sacred books, and wisest of men.

"Give, and you shall receive.'

And the teachings guide that whatever you give you will get back many times over; and that your giving will remain forever with them, and you. Both good things given, and bad things given.

The examples are so simple, but so clear.

If you are selfish, you will be shunned. If you are mean, you will be resented. If you bully, you will be disdained. If you are ungrateful, you be seen as thankless and selfish. If you are dishonest, you will be cast aside.

But if you are kind, people will treat you with kindness and compassion. If you are honest, you will be trusted. If you are courageous, you will be respected. If you care for people, they will care for you. And if you love, you will be loved.

They never end.

This is the simple yet powerful 'Truth'.

If you embed this 'Truth' into your brain, life, and soul, and employ this every single day with every single person you may meet or touch in anyway, it will change how you act and how you feel. And it will change how others view you, and how they feel about you.

It will change your life, and your world.

If you don't believe me, I dare you to give any person a genuine smile today.

You will be enlightened immediately, and see with your own eyes,

that a smile will come right back.

It is more than Magical…

It is Magic.

                                                                Leigh

'We make a living by what we get, but we make a life by what we give.'
Winston Churchill, British statesman and politician

BELIEVE IN

THE TRUTH
GIVING

Definition: to present voluntarily and without expecting compensation.

"For it is in giving that we receive.'
St. Francis of Asisi

IMAGINE A DAY

Imagine a day
Of just giving away
The whole world giving
A whole new way

One day, the whole world whole
Each, and every soul

Giving, wanting nothing in return
No one, saying
Now it's 'my turn'

Imagine this day, could it ever be real
Imagine
How the world might feel

It may be one word
A nod or a hand
It may be some time
To care, understand

It may be, to open a door
To feel real love
Not hate, or war

It may be a smile
All they may need
Or a meal, to heal
Maybe feed

Supporting a cause
Your money or time
It may be a million
Maybe a dime

That the giving happens, from the heart
Not a deal

It doesn't matter
What matters; it's real

'Give, and you shall receive.'
Luke

Cause giving with expectations
Isn't giving at all
It's taking, it's petty
It's just so small

Imagine a day when real giving took hold
Imagine how the world might change
Maybe mold

With a day like this
We would get so much
Not only from others
But from those we touch

Something from someone
Is nice indeed
But what we get from giving
Is special, a creed

You will get what you get
And get back what you give
Twice the feeling
It's the best way to live

If people like it, they might just say
Let's try this
Maybe one more day

Imagine if this day
Turned to two, or three
The whole wide world
On a giving spree

Imagine this day
If we dream and pray
It turned, somehow
To every day

A dream, perhaps
But there is more than one
There may be enough
To someday, become

Leigh

'Forgiveness is not an occasional act, it is a permanent attitude.'
Martin Luther King

BELIEVE IN

FORGIVENESS

Definition: to grant pardon for or remission of an offense; to cease to feel resentment.

'Love is an act of endless forgiveness.'
Peter Ustinov

THE FORGIVENESS TREE

I had this dream the other night. It seemed so real. The setting was surrounded by and within nature, the most authentic and soothing healing ground for all.

I invited my family, friends, and even some select others, to a gathering - in this open grassy field. The sun was bright with a deep blue sky, and there was a gentle warm breeze.

In the middle of this field, stood one large Oak Tree. I said softly, 'How about if we all just go and sit under that Tree?'

I began walking slowly, and everyone quietly followed.

I looked back and saw them all walking in an unattached straight vertical line – one behind the other, and all several feet back. Their faces seemed a bit uncomfortable, and all seemed to feel concerned and confused.

We got to the tree, and I asked everyone to sit down; and then looked up and simply said,

"This is so difficult for me to say out loud, but for those whom I have ever hurt, I would like to ask for your forgiveness. And to those who have ever hurt me, I would be pleased to accept your forgiveness."

I asked all to consider asking for the same, and then shared we could all do this without saying a word, because of this dream, The Forgiveness Tree.

It knows it takes courage to ask for Forgiveness in person – out loud and wide. It knows it is easier for people to feel, and so it privately shares feelings of those who want their feeling to be heard. If asked by those near it, the Tree will imbed forgiveness into their hearts and souls.

I asked that we all close our eyes, and each privately share and accept forgiveness in all its forms. I told them The Forgiveness Tree would do the rest, and magically share all offers and requests –

There was silence. and then all slowly closed their eyes.

And as I closed my eyes, I felt inside a little understood secret about forgiveness the Tree seemed to share with me…

We were all in a trance for a while, and then magically all eyes opened at one time. And we all got up and began slowly walking back - from whence we came.

I was in the lead and looked back.

I saw that arms were intertwined, and hands were being held. It was one big circle with each person attached to all others, left to right - side by side. And this large moving connected circle of people seemed to overwhelm the field. All faces were at ease with genuine smiles – and all seemed full of joy and peace.

And in that crowd, I also saw me.

Forgiveness enlightens and heals. For those who have the courage to offer and accept forgiveness, and all those around.

And as the Tree and all the holy books and wise men teach, to understand everything, you must forgive everything…

which includes that little understood secret I privately heard that Forgiveness Tree share with me…

In order forgive everything,

You must also forgive,

You.

Leigh

'Great things are done when men and mountains meet.'
William Blake

BELIEVE IN

OVERCOME

Definition: to get the better of in a struggle or conflict; to conquer; prevail; defeat.

'Your hardest times often lead to the greatest moments of your life.'
Roy T. Bennett

LOU PAULMIER

We walked into the large joyous room and looked across the floor.

There he was, sitting in a small wooden chair. Next to all the tables where the entire wedding party was sitting. He had been a teacher and wresting coach, and our camp counselor for so many years.

He was the Patriarch of the family. A great large Quaker family. One I had known, and looked up to, since I was 12.

He was sitting completely straight. Back like an arrow. Head high. Turning slightly to the left, and then to the right. Taking it all in. The leader of the band.

I noticed that he focused on Greg. His son, our good friend, who had earlier said his Vows.

And when I saw him across that long large hall, I saw complete pride, utter joy.

As my brothers and I slowly walked into the hall, full of a hundred people, his head turned toward the entrance where we were.

I saw his body move. Waiver a bit. Turn it toward us. It struggled to make sure we saw him. An invitation to say hello. A demand to say hello.

We walked toward him slowly; wanting to first see him, before any others.

As we slowly approached him, I saw him take hold of his cane. First with his right hand, and then awkwardly with his left. So he could use it as a lever to stand. I noticed no one offered to help him. And knew why. He didn't want help. He would not accept it.

As we met him, he was standing. A body which was not supposed to stand, but stood. Head held high.

A great big smile came across his face. It covered half his face. His moist eyes were full, of life.

We held out our hand, but he asked that we come closer. His arms trembled, moved upward, and shook. And as they somehow struggled to move up high, they came over my shoulders, until I was in his arms.

He did that to all three of us. My two brothers, and me.

'The greater the obstacle, the more glory in overcoming it.'
Moliere, French playwrite and author

After the hugs, he stood up straight, his body rocking uncontrollably, his head going back and forth. His joints contorted, his whole body tied in knots. He looked us straight in the eyes.

'Thank you,' he said. A thank you no one else might be able to understand, since his mouth, and face muscles, were not in his control. But a thank you that was so clear to us. A thank you he said four times, each etched into my mind. He did not just say it. He roared it. The whole room could hear. A loud inaudible Thank You. Completely at ease. Unembarrassed.

The Parkinson's he had lived with for 25 years, had taken its toll.

His body told him he could not stand, and his mouth told him he could not speak. But he stood straight, and he roared.

Although his body was not in his complete control, his mind, spirit, and soul were. He would not allow his body to trap them. He would not allow it, at all.

After our 'chat' of about 5 minutes, he sat back down, body shaking, with the assistance of his cane. He looked up at us one more time, with that smile which took over his face. He then pointed in the direction of Greg, letting us know it was now time for us to visit with him.

He was a man full of pride. Full of joy. A man I respected as much as any man I have ever known.

A man among men.

In a body which could not stand. With a mouth which could not speak. With a spirit which might not feel.

But he stood tall. He spoke proud. He felt deep.

Lou Paulmier exemplified what it means to stand and get up, rather than sit or stay down.

A person who defined that word 'overcome,' which is sometimes doing things you feel is so impossible, you just cannot do.

But Lou Paulmier was the type of person who didn't believe in that word 'impossible.'

He was the type of person who did things

a person just cannot do.

Leigh

'Gratitude is the parent of all virtues.'
Marcus Cicero

BELIEVE IN

GRATITUDE

Definition: To be warmly or deeply appreciative of kindness or benefits received; being thankful.

'Gratitude is the sign of noble souls.'
Aesop, ancient Greek philosopher

WORD TO BELIEVE: GRATITUDE

ROGER RANDALL AND SONS

I met Roger Randall about 20 years ago. He had put up a simple handwritten note on my door. It simply said he does handyman work, and was in town. Since we had a room that needed to be painted, I called him.

Since then we have used Roger in a hundred different ways. He has helped my brother and I build our real estate business from less than zero, to what it is today.

When I watch Roger, I notice the work of his agile hands, and mind. He carefully plans, measures, cuts, and just puts things together so skillfully - and with ease. He is fair, and has values, and honest as they come. He is responsive, quick, courteous, independent, and caring, and just somehow figures things out. And he, and now his son's and son-in-law - Roger Jr., Brian, and Jim – they never complain.

Their pants and shirts look tied died, with paint and dirt from days past. That is their 'uniform;' that and a baseball cap.

Those stuffy old ties and jackets I used to wear at 'the office' seem so silly now.

For some reason, I have always respected, been pulled toward, and feel more comfortable with those who work with their hands. They are 'real' people who know what is important and work at least ten to twelve hours a day. You can just feel they love their work - because it is theirs.

But one thing that has always struck me about them all, is that they always seem happy and grateful, which can't be taught. Those two words are a team. You cannot have one without the other. They just can't be pulled apart.

Gratefulness is the virtue of all virtues. I have learned that in order to be happy, you must be grateful. And in order to be grateful, you must be happy. That is proven, and a rule. I have never ever met even one person, who is happy and ungrateful – or vice versa. Not even one. Which means none.

I have also seen there is a calmness to a life lived in gratitude, a quiet joy.

And I can sense joy with Roger and his team.

These people are the type of people I like to hang around.

Those hardworking, authentic, grateful people,

with caring, agile, and calloused hands. Leigh

'Character, not circumstances, make the man.'
Booker T. Washington, American educator and author, who was at one time a slave,

BELIEVE IN

CHARACTER

'The most highly prized virtue of all honorable men, is character.'
Henry Clay

Definition: the aggregate of features and traits that form the individual nature of some person or thing

'When character is lost, all is lost.'
Billy Graham

JOHN TULP

We were in the middle of the Third Machias Lake, in the northern part of Maine. A beautiful lake, which only a few know. We were in our canoes. Seven of us, sitting there with our paddles up on top of the gutters. It was windless, and completely still. We were looking patiently at the same spot, towards this little bend. We were waiting for him, the last one of the band.

He told us he would meet us at our island campground around noon that day. So around that time, we all canoed out to the middle of the lake, and just sat and waited, looking for some sign of movement, around that far off bend. We knew he would appear,

because he said he would.

After a while, we saw some movement way off in the distance. We knew it was him. I looked at all the faces in those canoes and could see only smiles. The trip would not be the same, without him.

At one time he was my counselor. He was one of the first to teach me how to play tennis, which I play religiously to this day. For nearly 40 years, he had been a teacher at a private school in Massachusetts, teaching Latin, and much more. I have talked to many of his students, and they say he was a 'legend.' He has influenced, and impacted, hundreds, perhaps thousands, of kids.

One of them is me.

Rather than dictate and preach, he has this effortless way to guide, and share. His life is uncomplicated, and simple. There are no pretenses. He is a man who camps out and sleeps in a tree in the woods on the shores of lakes, in a simple $10 hammock, most summer nights. His old town canoe is the most expensive thing he owns. And he is the best fisherman in the world.

He is the Teacher. Those around him learn, as they simply watch. He is cultured and educated. He is poised, kind, honest, and mannered. He has integrity, is trustworthy, and smart. When he speaks, we all turn, and listen. He is his own man, a renaissance-type man.

And he has this most natural, authentic, and charming laugh.

He is a man who prefers to give, rather than receive. A man who thinks of others and makes a difference in how we all feel.

He lives his life, his own right way, and the right way with and for others.

'Character is doing the right thing when you are alone, with no one looking.'
John Wooden

He is a man so completely comfortable in his own skin,

because he knows, so completely, and totally,

what's underneath.

Leigh

'Three things in human life are important. The first is to be kind. The second is to be kind. And the third is to be kind.'
Henry James, Jr.

BELIEVE IN

KINDNESS

'One kind word can warm three winter months.'
Japanese Proverb

Definition: of a good nature or disposition, having, showing, or proceeding from benevolence; considerate and humane.

'One of the most difficult things to give away is kindness,
since it is always returned.'
Cort R. Flint

BOB LEMIEUX

It was Sunday, around 4:00 PM. I looked out the window. I saw him walking down our driveway, with a flower in his right hand. It was yellow. A rose, I think. Just one. Perfectly straight; wrapped in some kind of light wrapping paper.

He held it out ahead of him, walking briskly. Like he couldn't wait to get there. He was going over to give it to Alice, a neighbor, across the street.

Alice is one of the nicest people any person might ever have the opportunity to know. A person who makes you feel completely at ease. The type of person who is genuine; real. You can feel it.

He had known Alice for quite a while. As he had done consistently for years, he was going over to her place to pick her up for a date. A date that had been pre-arranged without them even arranging. He would just go there, and she would be eagerly waiting.

He had been in a car accident 20 years before. A severe head injury, which left him lifeless. Because of God's will, the ambulance arrived in time, and they somehow brought him back to life. His body broken in a hundred places, his brain bashed in. He had to learn to walk, talk, and think again. Slowly, after 20 years, he is now like you or me. He provided us all a lesson on a word called Will.

He has been our tenant for 25 years, living in the back part of our home; now a member of our 'family.' Although now in his fifties, he looks 10 years younger, because he takes such good care of himself.

With flower in hand, holding it outward, like it may break, I saw him cross the street. As he went up her driveway, his pace got a bit faster. He could not wait.

I saw Alice eagerly look out her kitchen window. She was so much looking forward to going to the bean supper at the church. There, they would be able to visit, be comfortable, and socialize with others they knew.

Before he got to the door, Alice had opened it. A big smile on her face, welcoming him in. Shortly thereafter, the door re-opened. They both started down the path toward her car. The path that, in the winter, Bob would shovel after each snow.

He had his right arm around her shoulder, and left hand under her elbow. Alice was leaning forward, supporting herself with her rolling walker and cane. Her knees were rocking. But Bob steadied her, and they slowly walked together toward the car.

'Kindness is its own religion.'
Dalia Lama

Two or three inches at a time.

You see, Alice is 92 years old.

Because of her age, Alice can't get out much anymore. She lost her husband, Rob, 10 years ago. He was just like her. There aren't many people 'there' for her anymore.

But Bob is there.

Bob, who remembers how it felt to be broken, and for others to care.

A kind and caring man, now whole in every way.

A man, who was lifeless 20 years ago.

But who now brings a flower, and life, to Alice each Sunday afternoon.

And to me, inside.

Leigh

'The family is one of nature's masterpieces.'
George Santayana

BELIEVE IN

FAMILY

Definition: a basic social unit consisting of one or more people considered as a group, whether dwelling together or not.

'Family faces are magic mirrors looking at people who belong to us.'
Gail Lumet Buckley

BUCKET

We live in a nice little town in southern Maine. A town called Yarmouth Village, near Portland. It is a great Village – it looks like all those Norman Rockwell paintings you sometimes see on walls.

Like many, we are within walking distance of the schools.

Years ago, beginning when our eldest son, Brendan, was in 3rd grade, he would walk up the road a bit to the crosswalk which leads to the Elementary and Middles schools. He would meet the town's 'Crossing Guard', who would carefully have Brendan and all those kids in town safely cross West Elm Street to a path leading to those schools.

The 'Crossing Guard's' name was 'Bucket,' and he was 86 years old.

His job was to make sure the kids cross the street safely, since there were cars that used that street each morning and late afternoon. Each early morning around 6:30 AM, he drove his car up to the crosswalk about ½ hour before anyone might come. He parked it just off the road near the cross walk, pointed it in the direction most cars tend to come. He sat in the driver's seat of that old car before the kids arrived and protected that cross walk like it was his life.

If someone went 16-mph in that 15-mph zone, Bucket would turn his lights on and off, frantically wave his hands, and honk his horn. And make people slow down.

No one was going to mess with that crosswalk. No one was going to mess with 'his kids.' For over 15 years - every school day - he was there. I don't ever remember him missing even one day. He treated all his 'crossing walk' kids, like they were his family.

I had always felt lucky to have a guy like Bucket guarding that crosswalk, and our kids. All parents in town did at the time. He just seemed to really care.

Although he took his job seriously, Bucket was also a genuinely good-natured man. With a big natural smile. You could just tell he liked to have fun. The kids could tell too. The kids could sense things like that, you know. And because he liked them so much, they liked him. Things are funny that way.

Sometimes, he took this old little yellow rubber 'ducky' from his pants pocket, pointed it at the kids, and squeezed it to make this kind of high-pitched noise. It wasn't that loud, since it was old, but it always made the kids giggle and laugh.

'Family is a little word, created by love.'
Proverb

He seemed to love how the kids reacted. And as they did, he laughed with that big, natural broad smile. And there was always this real twinkle in those 82-year-old eyes.

Although that old little yellow rubber ducky was somehow kind of brownish and dirty looking, and not as yellow as it once was, it still made that squeaky sound. It worked kind of just fine.

I always assumed he picked it up at the dump.

One night at dinner we were talking about Bucket, and our youngest son, Erik, mentioned that he and some of his friends were chatting with Bucket that day. One of them just happened ask Bucket where he lived, and if he had any children. Although a private man, he told them he lived in a small apartment on Main Street in town.

And then he softly mentioned he also was a father and Dad at one time.

He mentioned that he had one son,

but he passed away when he was only four years old.

He didn't share how his son had passed. I wasn't there, and so I don't know how he said it - but I do know he shared that most important piece of himself with my son and his friends that day.

And we also found out that he carried a piece of his son in his pocket each day.

We learned that when he pulled that old little dirty yellow rubber ducky from his right hip pants pocket, pointed it toward his 'kids', squeezed it, and laughed and smiled each day…

It was 55 years old.

It was his son's little yellow rubber ducky.

The little yellow ducky he squeezed to make his 'Crossing Walk' kids laugh and giggle, each day.

Like he remembered making his young son laugh and giggle,

55 years ago, each day.

Leigh

'Fish, cut bait, or get out of the boat.'
Old fisherman adage.

BELIEVE IN

WORK

Definition: exertion or effort directed to produce or accomplish something; labor; toil.

'Great things come from hard work and perseverance. No excuses '
Kobe Bryant

JEFF BUNT

We have this cabin up north, near this island, called Deer Isle, Maine. It is the lobster capital of the world. We go there every summer, and I have since I was 6. It is the nicest and most beautiful spot in the world. Anyone who has ever been there knows.

I have gotten to know a lot of the year-round people up there over the years. They are tough, and authentic. The 'real things.' One of those people is a guy named Jeff Bunt. I have known him for almost 15 years – but gotten to really know him the past 5 or so.

Jeff grew up in a home on Little Deer Isle adjacent to the home he is building for himself. He has lived in a trailer there for 15 years or so, but at the same time building a house near that trailer for - and by - himself. He decided to work on and finance it slowly on his own. He figured it wouldn't be too long before he would have his own lifetime home. He wouldn't owe anything to anyone then. He just likes it that way. That alone shows you he's much smarter than you and me.

Years ago, I gave him his first job cutting down a tree. He is now that only preferred 'tree guy' in all of Deer Isle and beyond. He is also lobsterman, a carpenter, a handy man, a caretaker, and mechanic - for boats, cars, and trucks. He has his own boats, and builds and services moorings, lobster traps, and docks. And he knows how to get rid of squirrels. He said he would take care of that for us, and by the end of the day all 40 of those squirrels in our cabin were gone. If fact, there are no longer any squirrels within 1000 yards of our home. He sent me pictures of how he did that, but that is a secret between only him and me.

But I think lobstering is what he loves most, pulling up traps and lobsters, alone with his son, Joshua, on that great shimmering Reach.

He and I have worked a lot together renovating my family's cabins up there – normally just he and I together, completely alone. A couple years ago he completely rebuilt our large family home, which was destroyed by water damage, and he essentially did that on his own. He also managed others in rebuilding that home, and they always did what he said, and when. His way with people is uncanny. But he doesn't even seem know that; it is all so natural for him.

As we cut wood, we measure things all the time. He typically just takes a pencil to a scrap piece of wood, makes an equation, and then the answer comes to him through the air. When we eat lunch together, sitting in saw dust on the porch, we both eat only peanut butter sandwiches – sometimes with Jelly and a pickle on top.

Do what you love. Know your own bone; gnaw at it, bury it,
unearth it, and gnaw it still.'
Henry David Thoreau

He tells me he buys things in bulk, because it is cheaper, and gives him a month's worth of food at a time. Like 20 large jars of peanut butter - as he points to the large peanut butter jar in his lap.

As we talk, and we talk quite a bit, I've learned he puts red beet juice in his tractor tires - so the tires don't freeze. One time he cut his metal trailer home in half with a saw, the one with a chain, so he could build the new house he is building where it needed to be. His has like 15 guns that he uses to hunt squirrels and keep the coyotes and wolves out of his yard, and feeds deer by hand each day since they come up to his driveway near his trailer home. He has named them, like most people name their dogs, but I just can't off-hand remember their names. And he 'potty trains' his dog by going out in the yard and peeing with him together as a team. It only took the dog 4 days to be potty trained that way.

I was about to asked how he trained him to take a dump, but thought the better of it, and didn't.

His yard has about 4-5 tractors, 3-4 trucks, 2-3 boats, and at least 500 lobster traps. With all sorts of other cool tools and big machine things that he uses for all his different types of work. I have absolutely no idea how he is able to do all he does.

Oh Yea….he is also funny as hell - and has this killer laugh.

But Jeff is more than all this or that.

He is a unique one and only type of guy, who can do anything and everything well - and seems to know everything too. He is true to his work, his word, and his friends. And loyal friends are rare and hard to find. I plan to write a book about Jeff – but that is for another time.

But the main thing I want to share about Jeff is about this word I call 'Hard Work'.

I cannot imagine even one person who could work harder than him. Not one. None. Which means zero to me. He works like 14 hours each day, 7 days a week – and doesn't take days off – never or ever.

And the unique thing about Jeff is that he doesn't just do great work, he also figured out how to make great work fun. When I work with him, we don't really work – but we get more than a ton of things done. With Jeff work isn't work, it is fun. It confuses me when I think about it at times.

Although I pay him to work with me, I am really working for him. Instead of me telling him what to do, he tells me what to do. He tells me when to be there - which is sometimes at early as 5 AM. We never stop when I am tired – because he never gets tired - we only stop when the work is done. Period on that.

'You are not your resume, you are your work.'
Seth Godin, Author

He also tells me when to do it, where to do it, how to do it, and why we are doing it. Instead of me being the boss, he is the boss.

We talk only when he says it is OK to talk, eat lunch when he says, stop work when he says, and never take breaks because he says. And even though I am older, I have learned a ton more from him, than him from me.

Jeff Bunt is a classic example on what 'Hard Work Ethic' can do. He knows things are earned, not given, and that work is the only real road that can take you to places you so dearly want to go.

He just works harder, longer, and smarter than others.

That is what the Harvard Business School types call his 'core competency' or 'differential competitive advantage.' People can sense and see that - eye to eye and ear to ear. And they want him to work both with and for them - all the time.

Normally when people work, things are built, and welded, into things.

but with Jeff Bunt, that word 'Hard Work,'

is built, and welded, deep into him.

Leigh

'Courage is a kind of salvation.'
   Plato

BELIEVE IN

COURAGE

Definition: the quality of mind or spirit that enables a person to face difficulty, danger, pain;
without fear; bravery.

'Courage is not the absence of fear, but rather the judgment that something else is more important than fear.'
Ambrose Redmoon

TRAVIS ROY

Last night our family went to hear Travis Roy speak at the Yarmouth High School auditorium. We had no idea what he might talk about, but somehow just wanted to go to hear him speak.

Travis grew up in Yarmouth. He was a standout hockey player; not only here, but in all of New England. He made the Boston University hockey team as a freshman. It was his lifelong goal. On October 20, 1995, eleven seconds into his first college varsity game, he fell into the boards, broke his fourth vertebrae, and his life was instantly changed.

Although now a quadriplegic with limited use of his right hand, Travis has graduated from BU, written 2 books, including the best seller Eleven Seconds, founded the Travis Roy Foundation for Spinal Cord Injuries, is fully employed, independent, and completely, and in every way, whole.

After he was done with his talk last night, he was given a standing ovation.

I stood up, and looked at others near me.

Unaware, my mouth was open, and my jaw was dropped. I noticed that the mouths and jaws of others were also open, and dropped. We just looked at each other, and nodded,

in awe.

It was only an hour, but it was one of the most touching and inspiring talks I had ever heard. It was not just what he said, but how he said it, with such grace, and poise. I am so glad we brought our two sons to listen.

He shared his experiences, and feelings, about where he had been, where he had gone, and where he now is.

He shared his feelings in the hospital bed, and how he cried like a baby when he got home. He remembers looking up from his bed at his Dad that night, and seeing the tears roll down his Dad's face too.

He shared what it was like when he first went back to BU, wheelchair bound; and the challenges and feelings he faced there.

But mostly he shared how he 'got through,' and words which struck a chord in us all.

'Courage is grace under pressure.'
Ernest Hemmingway

He said there are times when we choose our challenges, and times when challenges may choose us. It's about how we choose how to deal with them. It's about how we choose to overcome.

He believes, deeply, that attitude is infinitely important, and how you view things defines you.

He talked about how important goal setting is, and how it helped him move his hand to his mouth.

He talked about how important practice is, and how studying, and doing your best, is important, and cool.

He talked about pride, and how that drives who he is. He talked about character and values, and how they define what's inside.

He talked about family, and love, and how it is everyone's core.

And he talked about how lucky he felt.

He is a person who, quite simply, aspires and inspires.

His story is a story about character and courage only a few really know.

When someone asks me about a good role model for my kids to look up to, I know there are two words which will come to my mind, and from my mouth.

Those two words are

Travis Roy.

Leigh

'The most I can do for my friend, is simply to be his friend.'
Henry David Thoreau

BELIEVE IN

FRIENDSHIP

Definition: a person attached to another by feelings of affection or personal regard.

'A friend is one who walks in when the rest of the world walks out.'
Proverb

CHIP

Chip is our dog. He was named by Erik, our youngest son.

He is a Boykin Spaniel. It's a southern breed. Bred for hunting. But we don't hunt.

He is a cross between a Springer Spaniel, and Chesapeake Bay Retriever. He weighs about 40 pounds. He has dark wavy brown hair, bright green eyes, and the cutest head; with a blond streak on top.

We got him when he was only 6 weeks old. A little tiny thing. He is now 6. Although some in this breed are known to be a bit hyper, Chip is as calm as a completely still, windless lake, at dawn.

Except when he sees me, or one of 'us.'

Whenever I drive up to our home, I see Chip struggle to get out of his cuddled-up resting position. He is normally in his shallow-dug hole, under the bush in our front lawn. As I park, he wiggles off the dirt, shakes his head, and jogs to meet me.

As I get out, his tail is wiggling, and his body is jiggling.

He is so happy to see me. I just know he likes me. Actually, I just know he loves me. As if I am the only person in the world to him. The only thing that matters for him.

When I go inside, he follows me. I don't know why. But wherever I go, he follows. If I sit down on the couch in our living room, he lies at my feet. And when I get up to get a glass of milk, he follows me. And then follows me back. And again, he lies at my feet.

When there are times everyone else has gone to bed, and I am in my office, or on the couch, Chip is within 2 feet of me. When I decide to go to bed, he follows me, jumps up on our king-sized bed, and wraps himself up in the front left corner, touching my feet.

When I am in a melancholy or difficult mood, or when things haven't gone completely right that day, Chipper doesn't care.

He is there. Wiggling and waggling his tail and jiggling his body.

When there are days I feel no one else is there, Chipper is. He supports me. He doesn't bring me down. That, alone, makes me feel like gold.

'A friend is a gift you give to each other.'
Robert Lewis Stevenson

He loves me so much, I can't help but love him. He gets back from me, what he gives to me.

And a lot of food. Sometimes too much.

Chipper just seems to like me, for me. Not someone else I am not supposed to be. And I like him, for him. I can be myself with him. I can smile, my real smile. Nothing fake. All easy, natural, and real.

It's like a gift of some sorts, wrapped in a large bow-like ribbon.

I just trust him.

And like any real friend, I know he will be there, if I need him.

I know he will be there when others aren't.

Or if they leave.

Actually, like any truly real friend, those with the ribbons,

I know he will not just be there…

He will come.

Leigh

'Dare to be honest.'
Robert Burns

BELIEVE IN

HONESTY

"Be true to your work, your word, and your friend."
Henry David Thoreau

Definition: truthful; ethical; fair; not lying or cheating.

'Honesty is the first chapter in the book of Wisdom.'
Thomas Jefferson

HONESTY: A MINDSET

I was about 50 yards from the green. It was an important shot. All three of us bet lunch on this round. And we were even. Each one of us wanted that Grilled Chicken Salad.

Since I was the closest to the green, I had to wait for John and Dan to hit first.

I looked up quickly, and saw that Dan had swung; a divot, which barely touched the ball. It sputtered ahead about an inch or so.

Embarrassed for him, I pretended I didn't see. He didn't see me see him. And John was over a small hill, and couldn't possibly see.

A couple seconds later, I saw a ball in the air, a beautiful shot by Dan, inches from the hole.

I waited for John, who hit next. His too, was near the hole. And my shot was rare; close too. All three of us near that sacred hole.

We came up to the green, and started eying our balls. Looking ever so closely at our short lines to that tiny little hole.

"It looks like we may all end up in a tie," John said, incredulously

"I wish," said Dan, "but I am one shot behind both of you."

At that moment, with that little tiny thing,

I knew who Dan was.

Leigh

'To be trusted is a greater compliment than to be loved.'
George MacDonald, Scottish author and minister

BELIEVE IN

TRUST

'The best proof of love is Trust.'
Dr. Joyce Brothers

Definition: reliance on the integrity, strength, ability, surety of a person or thing.

'Trust is earned, respect is given, and loyalty is demonstrated.
Betrayal of any one of those is to lose all three.'
Buddha

TRUSTING YOU

Trust is defined as someone who is reliant, faithful, and sure. Someone who is obligated, caring, and dutiful. Someone who protects, safe-keeps, and guards. Someone with conviction. Someone who is honest and values their name.

It is the firm reliance on the integrity, ability, or character of a person.

Someone who is the Gospel Truth.

There are certain people in our lives who are special, and we would Trust with our lives. We know who they are and aren't.

And there are certain people who we look up to as role models. Those we do not know but view as people who define character and Trust. People like Nelson Mandela, Mahatma Gandhi, Mother Teresa, and Martin Luther King. And so many more….

These are people whose mere presence infuses Trust and Irreverence.

And we sometimes dream of being like them.

But the most important person in this world you know you need to Trust,

is You.

Because you can't Trust or be Trusted, if you don't first Trust you.

We strive to be able to look into the mirror, see an image looking back, and feel both good and at peace,

knowing we are looking at someone who infuses Trust, like them.

And so our dream comes true.

But you need to define and commit to your values, the Truth, and who you are and want to be.

And once you do,

You are somehow free.

Leigh

"As soon as you trust yourself, you will know how to live."
Johann Wolfgang Von Goethe

BELIEVE IN

PURPOSE

'The purpose of life is a life of purpose.'
Robert Bryne

Definition: the reason for which something exists or is done, made, or used.

'Extraordinary people start with purpose.'
Jesper Lowgren

BUCK

We have a cabin on Eggemoggin Reach in an area we call Down East, Deer Isle, Maine. I have been going there each summer since I was 6 years old. I consider it my sacred spot.

The people up there are as authentic as they come. One of them is one of my best friends, whom we all call 'Buck,' but whose name is Don. Most of us have known him since he was like 15 years old. He was the Principal of the Sedgewick Elementary School up there for 30 years. He even has a PHD, and prefers us to call him 'doctor.' But we don't.

Over the many summers up there, however, I have learned that he isn't just one of my best friends. He seems to also be one of the best friends of everyone else up there.

I talk to the guy who owns the little gas station and grocery store nearby, and his name comes up for no reason at all. I kind of brag to him that Buck is one of my best friends, but then he brags to me that Buck is one of his best friends. It's weird.

This same thing happens when I talk with the guy at the boat yard; Buck is one of his best friends, after I tell him he is one of my best friends. This same thing happens with the guy who stores my boat, and my electrician. And my plumber and my carpenter. And the guy that delivers the propane to our cabin, the guy who helps the guy who delivers that propane, all the ladies at the town Library, the guy who installed my internet, the guy who plows my driveway, the guy who mows my yard, and every single person who works at the Brooksville Town Hall. And even all of my many 50 relatives up there now know him 100 times better than they know me.

Yes, it's weird, and it kind of bothers me.

I also talk to people up there who are the ages of my kids. They not only know 'Mr. Buckingham,' but know him better than I do. They talk about him like he is their long-lost father or something.

Just the other day I mentioned Buck to this 22-year-old cashier at the grocery store, who was one of his students at the school. I bragged to her that he was one of my best friends. She went on to say how much she loved 'Mr. Buckingham,' and insinuated that he was her best friend. I was trying to figure out if she looked up to him as a role model - or had a crush on him. I even ran into the 12-year-old young daughter of a student he had, and even she was gushing about 'Mr. Buckingham.' Her mother, of course, was right there – nodding her head more than eagerly to agree.

'The meaning of life is to find your gift.
The purpose of life is to give it away.'
Pablo Picasso.

It's like 'The Stepford Wives', or something. It's weird. And yes, kind of bothers me for some reason. And I just couldn't figure this all out....

But over time, I did figure it out. And it as simple as - simple is as simple does.

Buck has always had a purpose driven life. We all need this in our lives since it gives us meaning. And the most important part of any definition of 'Purpose' needs to include a goal to 'make a difference' and have a truly positive impact on other's lives.

Although being a teacher, principal, and educator gave Buck the means to do this in very special ways, this didn't just happen because Buck was a school principal. It happened because of *how he was* a principal.

His purpose and goal weren't only to be a principal, but to make a difference and have a positive impact on and for others. This purpose defined how he would act, how he would treat people, and how he would feel. It was not confined to what he would do, but how he would live.

And he has obviously lived it incredibly well - because he has made that real difference, and positively impacted so many lives. All the people in and around the small town of Brooksville, Maine care for 'Buck' since he cared so much and so long for them. Things are funny that way.

It really is simple is as simple does.

We are all put on this planet for a reason, even though we may not understand or realize that for a while. Purpose isn't at all confined by what you 'do,' but rather how you live your life. It really gets down to how you choose to treat others and how you make them feel - and to be driven to make a difference and have a positive impact - somehow and someway - each day.

You could be an accountant, a brick layer, a painter, a banker, or a cashier - it doesn't really matter. And if you can't impact 100 lives, start by impacting just one. It is not the quantity, but quality of your impact that counts. If you change and improve the life of just one person in your life, that alone is an incredible feat.

If a person takes the time to define their own unique purpose, it can provide their life with genuine meaning and depth, and inspire others.

And so, one important purpose is to define your own unique purpose.

Because a life without purpose, is like a body without a soul....

'Buck' - Dr. Donald A. Buckingham Jr, of Sedgewick, Maine - is just one unique and very rare example of how just one person can positively impact

a whole town's soul.

Leigh

There is no such thing as a bad question.

YOUR QUESTION:

'Dad, what else do you believe?'

?

MY ANSWER:

'Whatever a person thinketh in his heart, so is he.'
Proverbs

I believe in, feel, and am

My Words

LAFFFF KEGHHH WWCCOPPDTTU.

MY ANSWER

'Dad, what else do you believe?' Who, really, are you?

There is this quote in a book in the bible called Proverbs which guides us to the beginning of the answer to your great question:

'Whatever a person thinketh in his heart, so is he.'

We are what we believe and feel in our hearts, that is who we are.

And so, I decided to define and prioritize those most important simple Words which reflected my core beliefs in my conscience and heart, and even write personal short stories about them to help me visualize them.

They are now imbedded within me. So much so that they guide me on what I do, how I act, treat others, think, and feel – and how others may view me.

I'd like to share them with you now.

Quite simply, I believe in, feel, and am these words:

First, and foremost, I believe in *Love* – especially Unconditional Love. Saint Mother Teresa's six-word quote sums it all up: 'Love is all there, really, is.' It really all starts and ends there. It is all that, really, matters.

I believe in *Attitude*. It defines how what we feel, and live, and in our complete control.

I believe in *Friendship*. Which are gifts, and some have ribbons.

I believe in *Family*. It is a little word, created by love.

I believe in *Forgiveness*. It heals those who forgive, the forgiven, and all those around.

I believe in *Faith*. I believe in something greater than me, and this feeling most call God. I have learned from the sacred books, teachings of wise men, and imbedding myself into nature. Over time, I have come to believe God is inside, not outside, each and all. That there is one God inside 8 billion names. Please believe and feel God is inside you, and *you* are one of his very important sacred names.

I believe in *Kindness*. Kindness is its own religion.

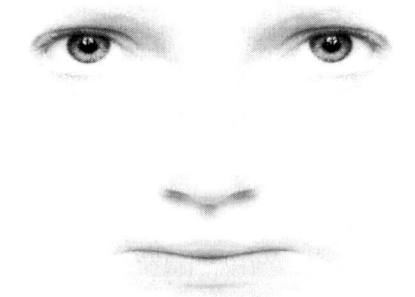

I believe in *Empathy*. Looking in the eyes of others - and seeing you.

I believe in *Gratefulness*. Appreciating just what we have.

I believe in *Honesty*. It is the first chapter in the book of wisdom.

I believe in *Hope*. You should never give or take it away. It may be all you or they have.

I believe in *Happiness*. Do not pursue it; create it. And it is so rewarding for you see other people being happy, because of you.

I believe in *Work*. You learn the value of work, by working hard.

I believe in the word *Wonder*. Wonder is the beginning of Wisdom. Always be curious.

I believe in *Character*. Doing the right things when no one is looking.

I believe in *Courage*. Doing things, you know you just cannot do.

I believe in *Overcoming*. It is all about getting up, after we all inevitably fall down.

I believe in *Poise*. Pose is Power. It is better to be an Eagle or Asprey, who glides and soar high, rather than a duck, which flaps and quacks and stays low.

I believe in *Purpose*. A life without purpose is like a body without a soul.

I believe in *Dreams*. Everything starts as somebody's daydream.

I believe in *Trust*. In order to trust or be trusted, You must first Trust You.

I believe in *The Truth:* What you give out, you will get back. Smile, and one will always come back. It's not magical, it's Magic.

And I Believe in *You*. The only person you are destined to become, is the person you decide to be.

> *But the greatest of these may be Faith, Hope, and Love - those only things which last forever – and are seared on my leg.*

I have memorized these words, and ingrained them into my heart, brain, and soul. It's empowering to know I can share them with others comfortably, and out loud. They serve as my sacred compass, which is buried within. And they guide how I live my life, act, treat others, and feel – and changed how others I touch may view me. My words are part of me and cannot be pried apart.

I am My Words.

'True happiness... is not attained through self-gratification,
but through fidelity to a worthy purpose'
Helen Keller

I am hoping you may take some of the Words I Believe and integrate them into the Words you decide to Believe - which will imbed your own compass within to guide your life, and those you touch. And to be able to comfortably articulate what you believe and feel, and who you are – only a very few can.

And with time, perhaps, you may share your Words and compass with your kids, and then, they may with theirs.

And so You, through your Words, live on in them, and theirs,

long after you are gone.

LAFFFF KEGHHH WWCCOPPDTTU.

Leigh

'There's a purpose and worth to every single life.'
Ronald Reagan

PROLOGUE TO STORIES

Topic	
Goals versus Purpose	164-169
Square Root of 24	170-171

'Clarify your Purpose, and you will be empowered.'
Jack Canfield

GOALS VERSUS PURPOSE

'The purpose of life is to be honorable, to be compassionate,
and to have it make some difference that you have lived and lived well.'
Ralph Waldo Emerson

GOALS VERSUS PURPOSE

Over the years, I was taught that in order to achieve, a person needs to set goals for themselves. Once set, goals will motivate, trigger behaviors, provide focus, and sustain momentum for you. Goals are set for you to achieve something for you.

This is good and right for you.

I have learned, however, that a person's Purpose is different. A Purpose should be centered on how a person makes a real difference and may make a positive impact on other's lives.

This is good for others, but also good for your soul.

Goals are centered on achievement and what you do. To and for me, however, a person's Purpose is quite different, and centered on how you live your life, and positively impact others' lives along the way.

Over the years I learned that if you integrate these two things, it can change how you think and feel, and imbed real meaning into your life. When younger, my goal was to build my own business so I could feel independent and free. In the beginning, like many others, my goal was focused on achievement. It wasn't based on a sense of any genuine 'Purpose', as I now know it to be, since I hadn't understood it at the time. I genuinely wish I had, and at times am burdened with regrets.

But as I got older and wiser, I learned more about 'Purpose,' and view it as a Mission Statement of sorts for a Life. And mission statements, I sense, like most things, should be simple and to the point.

My Purpose is private, but I will share it in the hopes it may provide some direction on what it means to and for me and could be for you. I have grown to feel I have two purposes. My first purpose is to love and care for my family. They are my deep core.

My second purpose, and I sometimes wonder why this couldn't be everyone's first or second purpose, is to somehow make others I touch in any way feel a bit better than if we hadn't touched that day. It may be a tone, a word, a compliment, a smile, or anything I may say or do to make them feel good or better even in any small way. And because I have experienced deep grief and pain, I especially have this need to comfort those who are struggling with suffering or adversity.

Not long ago, I was walking in Boston along a brick walkway, after dropping my son off at his college there. Looking ahead, I noticed a man ahead of me who was lying on the ground on the right-hand side of those bricks adjacent to a building.

'If you can't feed 100 people, feed just one.'
Saint Mother Teressa

As I got closer, I could see people looking down at him, but they all just walked by. 30 years ago, I too would have walked by. I know that because I had and did in past times. But now, because words like empathy, kindness, and purpose are engrained within, I have grown.

As I got near him, I could tell he was homeless, knowing he was probably struggling with addiction or mental illness. Instead of walking by, I knelt down to him on my knees to see how he was.

I found he was conscious, but not aware. And as I looked at his face, I saw me, or my kids. Because I know, but for the grace of God, that could easily be them or me.

I simply whispered in his ear, 'How are you doing?'

He flinched and seemed stunned that anyone would stop and care – because no one had. I told him everything was going to OK and then simply called 911 to let them know someone needed help. The police came quickly to take him to the Homeless Shelter nearby, and as they helped the man to his feet, he simply looked at me, and said, 'Thank you.'

I have found when you have really defined your compass and purpose deep within, you don't think.

You just do.

Your soul should guide your purpose,

and your purpose should follow your soul.

Leigh

'You don't have a soul. You are a soul. You have a body.'
Buddha

PROLOGUE: THE MOST IMPORTANT QUESTION

THE SQUARE ROOT OF 24

1. What is the square root of 24?

2. Who are you?

Both of these questions are answerable.

The answer to the first question is simply a formula, and you can find the answer on 'Google' in a second. The answer is 4.89.

The answer to the second question isn't a formula, and you can't find it on 'Google.'

But you can find the beginning of the answer in a book within the Bible called Proverbs:

"Whatever a person thinketh in his heart, so is he.'

Only we alone can answer that for ourselves, and define what is in our heart.

No one but you.

And the beginning of the answer may just be a matter of taking the time and work to define the words you believe, genuinely feeling them, practicing articulating them, ingraining them into your being and soul – which naturally imbeds a moral compass within which leads and guides you each day.

We spend most of our time studying and answering questions like that first one. But should we?

Which question, after all, could positively impact your life, directly impact how you live, act, treat others, and feel, and how others you touch may view you?

Would it be

'What is the square root of 24?'

Leigh

'The best thinking, is re-thinking.'
Shane Parrish

ADDENDUM

Topic	Page
Believe in the word Flexible *Other Words to Believe*	174-175
Believe in Practice *How to articulate and share what you believe, and who you are Out loud, and clear.*	176-177

'In life we cannot avoid change, we cannot avoid loss.
Freedom and happiness are found in the flexibility
and ease with which we move through change.'
Buddha

BELIEVE IN THE WORD FLEXIBLE

CHOOSE YOUR OWN WORDS TO BELIEVE

'A tree that is unbending is easily broken.' Lao Tzu

BE YOU

WORD	QUOTE
Grit	'The stubborn refusal to quit'
Loyalty	'Be loyal to what you love'
Dream	'If you can dream it, you can do it'
Self-Discipline	'The only discipline that lasts, is self-discipline'
Trust	'To be trusted, is a greater compliment than to be loved'
Manners	'Good manners will open doors the best education cannot'
Freedom	'Freedom is the oxygen of the soul'
Health	'A healthy outside starts from the inside'
Learning	'Yearn to Learn'
Practice	'Excellence is not an art. It is the habit of practice'
Patience	'Patience is sometimes bitter, but its fruit is sweet'
Smile	'Peace begins with a smile'
Service	'To find yourself, you must lose yourself in servicing others'
Commitment	'Commitment is an act, not a word'
Inspire	'You have incredible power when you inspire'
Alive	'Being alive, means loving being alive'
Joy	'Joy is a net of love by which you can catch souls/
Confidence	'Confidence allows you to do it'
Imagine	'Everything you can imagine, can be real'
Creativity	'Creatively is contagious and courageous; pass it on'
Believe	'What you believe, you receive'
Passion	'People with passion can make the impossible happen'
Opportunity	'Don't wait for opportunities; create them'
Excellence	'Excellence is not a skill; it is an attitude'
Challenge	'Don't limit your challenges, challenge our limits'
Determined	'Do not underestimate the determination of a quiet man'
Dare	'Only those who dare may fly'
Nurture	'Nurture your mind with great thoughts'
Fulfillment	'Happiness is the state of fulfillment, not gratification'
Adapt	'We cannot change the wind, but we can adjust the sails'
You	'Believe in You'

'The measure of intelligence is the ability to adapt, be flexible, and to change.'
Albert Einstein

'Don't practice until you get it right. Practice until you can't get it wrong.'
John Wooden

BELIEVE IN THE WORD PRACTICE

HOW TO MEMORIZE AND ARTICULATE YOUR WORDS

A Simple Lesson on Memory
How to remember and practice your words

Over the years, I have used a memory technique to help me retain information and memorize - and then share ideas.

With this method I create a new word or group of words by taking the first letter of each word in that group and linking or putting them together. For example, the first four words which I have chosen as words I want to embed into me may be Love, Attitude, Forgiveness and Faith.

The first four letters of those words are LAFF.

With practice, a person remembers the letters LAFF.

L: is linked in our brain as Love
A: is linked in your brain as Attitude.
F: is linked in your brain as Forgiveness, and
F: is linked in your brain as Faith.

I remember LAFF, and will think of Love, Attitude, Forgiveness, and Faith. With practice, each letter will link my brain to a word, and that will then link me to the meaning or story of that word, which helps me remember and share. And with practice I can do this with 3-4 different sets of words at a time. Mine, for example, are LAFFFF KEGHHH WWCCOPPDTTU. I know each word for each of those letters.

Practice will engrain your words and what you believe and feel into your brain, being, and soul, and you will be able to share your beliefs confidently for you, but also with others, and yours – because until you are able to articulate something with grace and clarity, you don't really know it.

But once you are able to, it will surprise and shock people – perhaps even you - since so few can.

Knowing what you believe, and who you are, *and being able to articulate that, out loud and clear,* cultivates and clarifies your own private internal compass.

And when that is in place, you really do become your own unique You.

'Your vision will become clear only when you can look into your own heart. Who looks outside, dreams; who looks inside, awakes.'
Carl Jung

ARISTOTLE'S WISDOM

'The most important relationship we can all have is the one you have with yourself.

The most important journey you can take is one of self-discovery.

To know yourself, you must spend time with yourself,

you must not be afraid to be alone.

Knowing yourself is the beginning of all wisdom.'

Aristotle
Ancient Greek philosopher and scientist, whose mentor was Plato, and who was one of the greatest intellectual figures of Western history

'All the Wonders you seek…

are within Yourself'

Thomas Browne

WORDS TO BELIEVE
AND *FEEL*
WORDS THAT DEFINE WHO PEOPLE ARE

'Dad, what else do you believe?'

'Whatever a person thinketh in his heart, so is he.'

'I believe in, feel, and am my words.'

May I ask you

What you believe, and feel?

May I ask you

Who are you?

Or want to be.

Actually, may I dare you to try to answer that question,
out loud, clearly, and comfortably.

For you, and yours, not me.

You may find, it may change you.

Made in the USA
Columbia, SC
27 April 2024

6b5c05c6-008e-42e0-b719-a60953b89233R01